TITLE

WELLNESS REIMAGINED: CANNABIS, DIGITAL INNOVATION, AND THE FUTURE OF HEALTH

SUBTITLE

A REVOLUTIONARY GUIDE TO NAVIGATING THE NEW FRONTIERS OF PERSONAL WELL-BEING

AUTHOR

RAUL CRISTIAN SĂRARU

This goes to our DQA team

RAUL C. SĂRARU | COPYRIGHT © 2024
ALL RIGHTS RESERVED

BEYOND BOUNDARIES

ABOUT THE AUTHOR

Raul Cristian Săraru is a visionary entrepreneur, author, and thought leader at the forefront of blending traditional wellness with the cutting-edge possibilities of digital innovation.

With a rich history of pioneering in diverse fields— from the entertainment industry to groundbreaking ventures in cannabis, crypto, and beyond — Raul's journey is one of continuous transformation and resilience.

Born with an innate curiosity and a relentless drive for exploration, Raul has navigated the tumultuous waves of various industries, each time emerging with invaluable insights and innovations.

His first book, "Navigating the Adult Industry, Cannabis: Crypto and Beyond," not only chronicles his unique path through these dynamic sectors but also serves as a testament to his adaptability and foresight in recognizing and harnessing the potential of emerging technologies for transformative purposes.

ABOUT THE AUTHOR

In "Wellness Reimagined: Cannabis, Digital Innovation, and the Future of Health," Raul embarks on a new chapter, delving into the synergies between cannabis, psychedelics, artificial intelligence, and blockchain technology within the realm of healthcare and wellness.

This work reflects his deep-seated belief in the power of holistic health practices, augmented by the precision and personalization afforded by digital technologies.

It's an invitation to readers to envision a future where health and well-being are not just managed but enhanced through a seamless blend of ancient wisdom and modern innovation.

Through his books, Raul aims to inspire others to embrace change, challenge the status quo, and join him on a transformative journey towards a healthier, more enlightened future.

CONTENT

The Evolution of Wellness - From Traditional to Transformative Therapies **1**
- Overview of the current state of Wellness and alternative therapies.
- Introduction to the book's goals and what readers can expect.

Cannabis at the Forefront of Wellness **2**
- A detailed exploration of Cannabis, its role in modern wellness, therapeutic applications.
- Understanding how alternative therapies are being recognized and integrated into healthcare systems.

The Rise of Psychedelics and AI in Medicine **3**
- Psychedelics for mental health treatment, supported by recent research and case studies.
- Explaining the use of AI in healthcare and its benefits for personalized treatment plans.

Digital Innovation in Wellness: Blockchain, NFTs and Beyond **4**
- How NFTs are being used in healthcare.
- The potential future uses of blockchain and digital assets in wellness.

Cannabis Expansion in Europe **5**
- Challenges and opportunities related to the expansion of Cannabis in Europe.
- Discussion on the ethical implications of these advancements.

The Road Ahead **6**
- Predictions for the future of wellness and healthcare.
- Final thoughts and reflections on how individuals and society can prepare for these changes.

Conclusion **7**
- Summary of key points.
- Closing thoughts on the importance of embracing technology for a healthier future

CHAPTER 1

The Evolution of Wellness - From Traditional to Transformative Therapies

On this path of personal transformation, I've seen how Cannabis has moved from being doubted to becoming a key player in medicine, bringing relief new possibilities for countless individuals. 'Speaking' directly to you, my dear reader, this shift from being questioned to welcomed really highlights how we're all starting to see the value of natural remedies in taking care of our health.

In this changing environment, Cannabis has risen from a backdrop of debate to shine as a pioneer of medical progress, bringing hope and alleviation to many. Its journey from criticism to acceptance is a testament to our shifting perspectives on plant-based medicines and their legitimate role in the Healthcare Ecosystem.

At the same time, we're witnessing a renewed examination of Psychedelics, previously dismissed due to social prejudices, indicating a wider willingness to consider all possible mental health treatments. Innovative studies on compounds such as Psilocybin are revealing new opportunities to confront some of the most challenging mental health issues, offering hope to those who've found traditional methods insufficient.

CHAPTER 1.2

Intertwined with these developments is the rise of Artificial Intelligence in healthcare, which offers tools to customize treatment in previously unimaginable ways.

AI's skill in analyzing and learning from extensive data is leading us into a revolutionary healthcare era. Now, we're moving beyond just tackling symptoms to enhancing overall well-being, with treatments meticulously customized for you.

"Wellness Reimagined: Cannabis, Digital Innovation, and the Future of Health" is not an Academic exploration but a continuation of my own personal Odyssey. Set against the backdrop of the digital revolutions reshaping our future, it represents a new chapter in a story of growth where technology meets traditional healing.

With the start of the Digital Quantum Association (DQA), my path gained new depth. The DQA's goal, blending the Cannabis Industry and Blockchain Technology, strives for a more unified and holistic way of living.

This mission is underscored by the lessons of the past, teaching us resilience and adaptability as we build a road that paves the way to future wellness through personal and professional upheavals.

CHAPTER 1.3

My journey, a testament to the power of reinvention as chronicled in "Navigating the Adult Industry, Cannabis, Crypto, and Beyond," mirrors this broader shift.
It is a narrative steeped in transformation, detailing my voyage from the complexities of my previous industry to the pioneering frontiers of Cannabis and
Blockchain Technology.
This journey, marked by resilience and adaptability, has been anything but linear.

Digital Quantum Association | Ecosystem

CHAPTER 1.4

As I explore the depths of Psychedelic Medicine and the cutting-edge role of Artificial Intelligence in Healthcare, I find myself at a crucial turning point. This is the moment where ancient wisdom and modern innovations merge, envisioning a future where Wellness forms a unified, personalized, and Holistic spectrum, open to everyone.

This book is my invitation to you to step out of the ordinary and into a realm where health and well-being are transformed by the powerful combination of technology and age-old healing practices.

I urge you to seize the opportunities that emerge at the intersection of wellness and technology, venturing into uncharted territories of health and healing equipped with knowledge that could dramatically alter how we live our lives for the better.

As we venture into this journey together, it's clear to me that achieving wellness is both a personal quest and a shared mission. It goes beyond unraveling the complexities of healthcare; it's about setting a path towards a future where each of us can reach our highest potential for health and joy.

CHAPTER 1.5

Let us journey onward, inspired by the tireless efforts to make the World a healthier, more connected place.
I'm heading towards a future that goes beyond the everyday, enlightened by the glow of breakthroughs and the steady courage of Humanity.

"Wellness Reimagined: Cannabis, Digital Innovation, and the Future of Health" isn't just a book; it's my call to you to embark on a transformative exploration that reshapes what Wellness means in our digitally evolving era.

CHAPTER 2

Cannabis at the Forefront of Wellness

Did you know that the Endocannabinoid System, which runs throughout our entire body, is a feature shared by all of us Humans and every other Mammal out there? It's a fascinating scientific fact mentioned in every medical textbook on the Planet and taught in medical schools Worldwide. Just let that sink in for a moment!

The fact that Marijuana has come from being seen as an evil and taboo substance to serve as a beacon of hope for many who suffer from a wide range of illnesses, all over the World, is yet another indicator of a continuously evolving understanding of just what constitutes effective, compassionate healthcare.

The Therapeutic Renaissance of Cannabis

Maybe the most striking story in Wellness right now is how Cannabis is making a comeback as a healer. This plant has a rich history in ancient medicine, and today, it's experiencing a revival.

Conditions such as chronic pain, epilepsy, anxiety, and insomnia most of the time are considered beyond treatment; now, they are beginning to be approached with new hope through cannabis treatments.

CHAPTER 2.1

"Cannabis: A Lost History" is a documentary that digs deep into the untold stories of a plant that's been crucial to human culture, medicine, and spirituality for centuries.

In recent years, research has really boosted our knowledge of how Cannabis works with the body's Endocannabinoid System.
This system is a web of receptors vital for maintaining balance in our bodies.

Check out "The Endocannabinoid System" on Aurora Europe's YouTube channel. The video breaks down the science of cannabis in a way that's easy for anyone to understand.

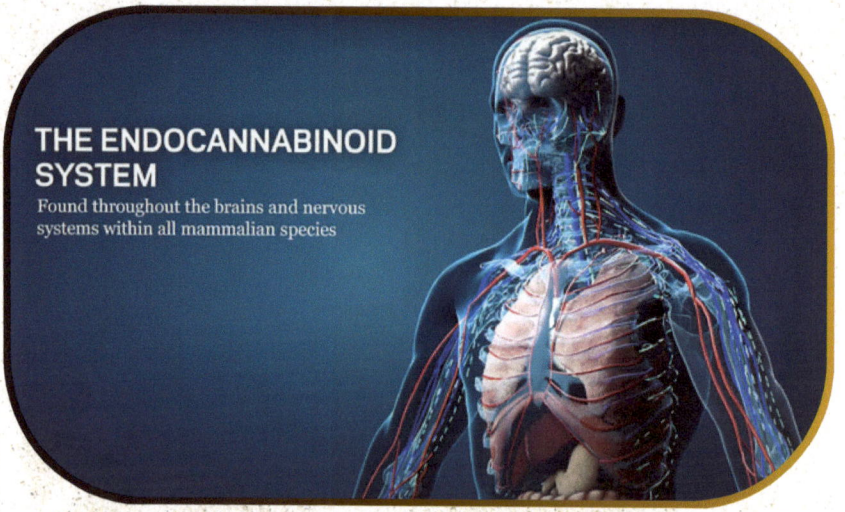

CHAPTER 2.2

"The Endocannabinoid System" video by Aurora Europe demystifies how cannabis works within the body. This piece of content, presented by a top distributor of medical cannabis in the European Union, is perfect for anyone looking to understand the science of cannabis in an easy-to-digest format.

Through what I've learned, cannabinoids like **THC** and **CBD** are proving to be breakthroughs for a wide range of symptoms and conditions. This represents a significant shift in our understanding and application of this plant in health and wellness - a shift I believe is crucial for you to understand my dear reader.

It's worth noting that the Association (**DQA**) I founded is deeply involved in every aspect of this flourishing field, from research and education to the distribution and application of cannabis-based solutions.

Most importantly, the therapeutic use of cannabis has had a tremendous impact on our lives, clearly showing us the potential of this plant to transform lives and offer safer, more sustainable approaches to managing pain and symptoms.

CHAPTER 2.3

Case Studies: Real-World Impacts

Without delving into countless of examples, academic or otherwise, I've intentionally chosen two common cases that have had a tremendous impact on me, especially considering my personal ordeal — a journey detailed extensively in my previous Book.

Kara Zartler - Relief from Cerebral Palsy and Severe Autism

Mark Zartler, from Richardson, Texas, takes a step few parents might think of. He risks a lot to help his daughter, Kara, manage her severe cerebral palsy and autism. No prescription seems to give the poor child relief from her symptoms, including the self-harm that comes with her intense behavioral outbursts.

The Zartlers' discovery of cannabis as a therapeutic agent marked a turning point. Mark found that vaporized cannabis provided immediate and noticeable relief for Kara, reducing the frequency and severity of her symptoms.

CHAPTER 2.4

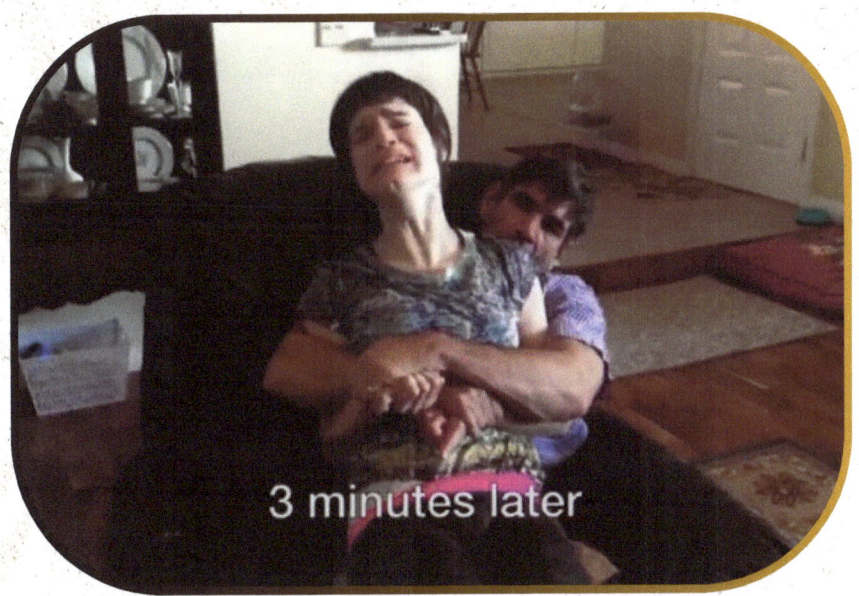

This case was widely shared, including a detailed account on YouTube, offering a touching look at the struggles many families face and the lengths to which they'll go to find relief for their loved ones.

For a more detailed look into Kara's story, a video titled "Richardson father risks freedom to promote cannabis treatments for his daughter" is available on YouTube, providing an intimate glimpse into the Zartler family's journey. You must see it for yourself!

I follow her on Facebook, where she last posted a photo with her mom for Christmas on December 20th, 2023, last year.

CHAPTER 2.5

Larry - Combatting Parkinson's Disease Symptoms

Another remarkable instance of cannabis's therapeutic potential is seen in the experience of Larry, a retired police captain battling Parkinson's disease. Traditional medications did little to ease his tremor dyskinesia and voice issues, which significantly impacted his quality of life.

The documentary **"Ride with Larry"** captures the moment Larry tries medical marijuana for the first time, with the results being nothing short of astonishing. The footage shows a dramatic reduction in tremors and an improvement in Larry's speech, underscoring the potential of cannabis to alleviate symptoms of Parkinson's disease.

This moment, available for viewing on Amazon and highlighted on YouTube, showcases the immediate and profound impact cannabis can have, offering hope and evidence of its benefits for those living with Parkinson's.

"Ride with Larry" provides a comprehensive view of Larry's journey and the effects of cannabis on his Parkinson's symptoms. Facebook page

CHAPTER 2.6

"Where do you find the strength to live when you suffer an incurable disease?

After a 20-year battle with Parkinson's, Larry refuses to give up and will attempt the unthinkable: a 300-mile bike ride across South Dakota, a journey of hope for anyone facing a life altering illness.

In this intimate portrait of courage, love, and community, Larry will prove that if you love life, you fight for it."

In memory of Larry, who, after inspiring me and many others, sadly passed away in 2020. For more details, please see this [report](#).

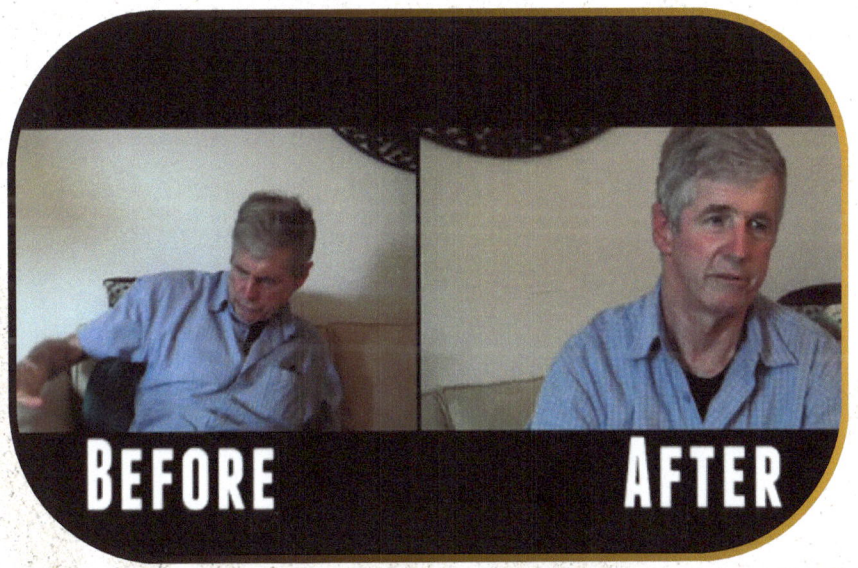

R.I.P. Captain Larry Smith

BEYOND BOUNDARIES

CHAPTER 2.7

Integration into Healthcare Systems

The growing acceptance of cannabis marks not just a cultural shift but also a transformation within healthcare systems around the world. Nations everywhere are revisiting their stance on cannabis, leading to more medical applications for it.

We're seeing more healthcare professionals acknowledge cannabis's role in comprehensive treatment methods, sparking conversations on how to weave it into our treatment plans and healthcare strategies.

Yet, integrating cannabis into healthcare isn't without its hurdles. Issues like regulatory obstacles, limited access, and the ongoing need for research are significant challenges we face together.

Despite these obstacles, the path cannabis is on as a treatment option, looks incredibly hopeful. Continuous research and changes in policy are laying the groundwork for its wider acceptance and understanding among us all.

CHAPTER 2.8

The Future of Cannabis in Wellness

Thanks to technological breakthroughs, the crafting of specific cannabinoid treatments, and our expanding insight into its health perks, cannabis is on the brink of revolutionizing our approach to health and wellness, making it more whole and tailored than ever before.

Join me in this exploration, and let's embrace the changes and opportunities the next chapter will reveal to us.

In a future where the skyline is lit by the verdant glow of cannabis-inspired architecture, we venture into a realm where wellness and technology intertwine, crafting therapies as advanced as the society that embraces them.

CHAPTER 3

The Rise of Psychedelics and AI in Medicine

The treatment landscape of mental health is changing remarkably due to the renaissance of Psychedelic research and the use of Artificial Intelligence (AI) in healthcare. Recent research and evidence have supported a revival in interest in the use of psychedelics to treat many kinds of mental illness.

In this chapter, we'll dive into how AI is revolutionizing personalized medicine, paving the way for a future where research in both Cannabis and Psychedelics is enhancing and broadening treatment options.

Psychedelics: A New Dawn in Mental Health Treatment

The comeback of psychedelics in mental health research is truly changing the game, moving away from old stigmas and positioning these substances at the cutting edge of treatment options.

Today, serious studies are focusing on Psilocybin, LSD, and MDMA, offering new hope to those who haven't found much success with traditional treatments. These substances are now being explored as potential lifelines for tackling tough mental health challenges like depression, PTSD, and the anxiety that comes with facing life-ending illnesses.

CHAPTER 3.1

Recent changes in Australia's laws, making it legal to use psychedelics for treating depression and trauma, highlight their recognized healing power.

This groundbreaking decision, deeply explored in <u>ABC News</u>' "Using psychedelics to treat depression and trauma," offers both hope and a word of caution. It's a story that also reveals how some, driven by a deep need for relief, seek these treatments even when it's not fully legal.

The narrative also touches upon individuals seeking these treatments outside the bounds of legality, driven by the urgent need for relief and healing.

The stories of Tim Baker, turning to an underground source for MDMA therapy to ease his end-of-life worries, and Vietnam veteran Roger Priest, who's looking forward to legally using psychedelic-assisted therapy for PTSD, show the varied journeys towards healing that people are embarking on.

Indira Naidoo presents this exploration, shedding light on the complex world of psychedelic research and therapy happening in Australia, inviting us to consider the wide spectrum of healing possibilities these substances offer.

CHAPTER 3.2

This reflects a worldwide shift, viewing psychedelics not merely as substances but as keys unlocking new approaches in mental health treatment.

The dynamic realm of psychedelic therapy — with its studies, individual trials, and legal changes — hints at a deeper reevaluation of what truly effective and caring treatment can be.

As we delve deeper into this field, our strong hope in the potential of psychedelics must go hand in hand with detailed scientific research and thoughtful ethical considerations. Only then can these powerful substances truly aid those battling mental illnesses.

We're all part of this unfolding story, exploring the vast possibilities psychedelics offer for healing, growth, and understanding.

Together, let's approach this journey with open hearts and eager minds, ready to discover the transformative power psychedelics hold.

CHAPTER 3.3

Being open and personal, I want to deepen the conversation about healing that we're diving into with this book.

The stories shared by the incredible people in the ABC News documentary are completely real.

My personal encounters with these substances in my younger days lay the groundwork for the professional insights I share with you. Without those experiences, I wouldn't be discussing this subject.

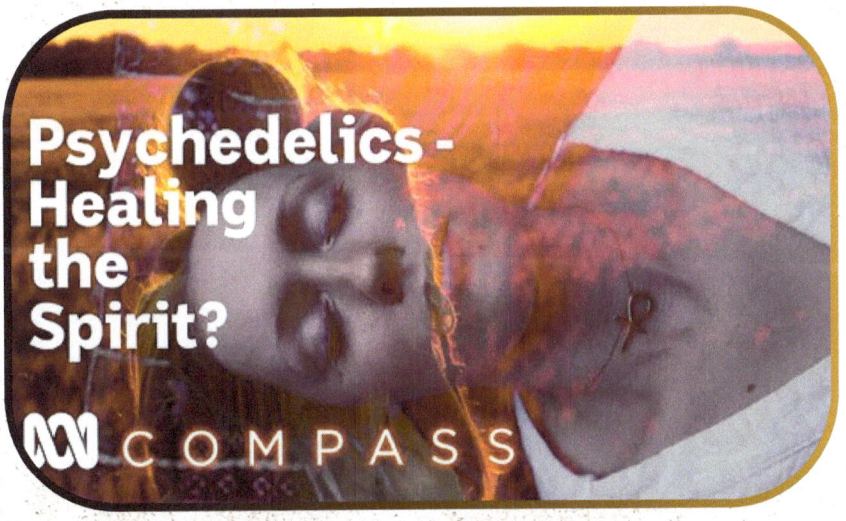

CHAPTER 3.4

Ayahuasca

Ayahuasca is a traditional South American brew with deep roots in the spiritual and healing practices of Amazonian indigenous peoples.

It's a mix made from the **Banisteriopsis caapi** vine and the **Psychotria viridis** leaf, the latter of which contains N,N-Dimethyltryptamine (DMT), a potent psychedelic compound. The **caapi** vine acts as an **MAOI** (Monoamine Oxidase Inhibitor), allowing the DMT to become orally active by preventing its breakdown in the digestive system.

This brew has been a key part of spiritual, cultural, and healing rituals for possibly thousands of years. It's used to unlock personal insights, heal emotional wounds, and connect deeply with the spiritual realm, often leading to transformative and profound experiences. It is known for inducing visions and introspective psychedelic experiences that users often describe as life-changing.

Drinking Ayahuasca isn't easy; it can cause nausea, vomiting, and other intense effects, which are seen as necessary for the cleansing and healing process by those who use it traditionally.

CHAPTER 3.5

The visions and emotional breakthroughs Ayahuasca triggers can deeply **'enlighten or unsettle'**, underscoring the importance of being guided by seasoned Shamans, and their teams of healers and practitioners.

As Ayahuasca's appeal spreads beyond its South American roots into alternative medicine and spirituality worldwide, its legal status remains complex, influenced by **DMT**'s regulation.

Yet, despite these hurdles, Ayahuasca retreats are on the rise, drawing people globally in search of healing, growth, and spiritual clarity.

While I haven't embarked on this journey myself, I've done my research and feel ready to take this step. I'm leaning towards seeking the wisdom of a Shaman and their healing team at **SpiritQuest | Ayahuasca & Huachuma Healing Center** (San Pedro), renowned since 1995.

Discover more about their work at SpiritQuest, joining us as we explore paths to healing and understanding.

CHAPTER 3.6

I recommend checking out Aubrey Marcus's video "Ayahuasca With 'The Dragon of The Jungle'" on his YouTube channel.

I really respect Marcus's work and suggest you follow him too. He shares his Ayahuasca journey, led by someone he calls "The Dragon of The Jungle."

The video gives a detailed look at his life-changing experience, showing us the powerful effects Ayahuasca can have on someone's personal development and
healing journey.

CHAPTER 3.7

GAIA

The original painting Acrylic and Ink on board (55×66 cm-2016 Budapest)

Knowing what you now know about my journey, my dear reader, you can imagine that I wouldn't choose anything but something spiritual and meaningful for our NFT series.

Please meet the artist who painted the original: **Kay Roy** - a dear brother, representing the DQA team proudly in the Interview he gave us.

CHAPTER 3.8

Artificial Intelligence: Customizing the Path to Wellness

Shifting our focus, we delve into Artificial Intelligence (AI), a transformative power reshaping healthcare. AI introduces unprecedented tools for tailoring treatment plans to individuals, a leap forward in medical personalization.

Beyond the realm of Psychedelic therapy, AI's insights allow for treatments to be finely tuned to each person's unique psychological and biological characteristics, leading to improved outcomes and reducing the guesswork often associated with psychiatric care.

AI's capabilities extend to predicting how well patients might respond to treatments, continuously tracking patient progress, and using health data patterns to pinpoint those who could benefit most from any kind of therapy.

This level of personalization is crucial, ensuring that every intervention isn't just effective but perfectly suited to meet each person's particular health needs and life situations.

CHAPTER 3.9

The Synergy of Psychedelics and AI in Medicine

The merging of psychedelics and AI in medicine marks an extraordinary moment, creating a new avenue for mental health care. This unique combination brings together the time-honored insights of psychedelic therapies with the advanced possibilities enabled by Artificial Intelligence.

This partnership aims to deliver treatments that are both highly effective and customized, enhancing the mental health field with nuanced, individualized solutions.

Dive into the cosmic dance of AI and psychedelics, a visionary gateway to healing that merges the wisdom of the ancients with the promise
of the future, opening new realms of compassion and care in the journey towards wellness.

CHAPTER 3.1.0

Yet, 'speaking' personally, I'm cautious about diving too deep into this subject right now. According to our <u>Whitepaper</u>, the Digital Quantum Association (DQA) suggests a more careful approach regarding how much we disclose about our strategic plans at this moment.

The concept of combining Psychedelics with AI in healthcare is indeed thrilling and distinct, warranting its own focused discussion — perhaps a topic for another book entirely.

While this topic fits perfectly with DQA's ethos, it demands more investigation than we can offer right now. Yet, it's important to acknowledge that we're on the brink of a new era in medicine, one that certainly deserves a thorough conversation in the near future.

Conclusion: A Future Transformed

We're heading towards a healthcare world where every part of what we feel and think is acknowledged and addressed with the compassion and cutting-edge solutions it genuinely deserves.

Now, with eager curiosity, let's jump into the next exciting part of our exploration, ready to discover the amazing opportunities that lie ahead.

CHAPTER 4

Digital Innovation in Wellness: Blockchain, NFTs and Beyond

Blockchain and **NFTs** represent more than technological breakthroughs; they embody the potential for profound shifts in how we access, interact with, and
benefit from healthcare.

GAIA NFT #10

CHAPTER 4.1

As I blend Digital Tech with Wellness, I'm excited to share how these advancements offer us the thrilling potential to make healthcare more private, personalized, and empowering for us as patients.

As we venture into the next chapter, I invite you to join us on a journey from traditional healthcare to a futuristic landscape where technology reshapes our understanding of wellness, a journey that's particularly meaningful to our Team at Digital Quantum Association (DQA).

In this exploration, we're delving into groundbreaking innovations — from Blockchain to NFTs and more — that are revolutionizing medicine and improving lives.

Among these, our **GAIA NFT** Collection stands out, embodying our commitment to leveraging technology for greater health and happiness, illustrating the profound impact these digital advancements have for us at DQA.

CHAPTER 4.2

Understanding Blockchain and NFTs

Our exploration now digs into the bedrock of these technological marvels — Blockchain Technology. At its essence, blockchain is a decentralized ledger, an innovative method for recording transactions or any form of digital interaction in a manner that is secure, transparent, and immutable.

This immutability means that once something is engraved into the blockchain, it remains unaltered and permanent, fostering a level of trust and verification that is unparalleled. For us in healthcare, this translates into unmatched security and integrity for medical records, guaranteeing that our personal health information stays confidential and clean.

NFTs, or Non-Fungible Tokens, further expand blockchain's application in wellness. Unlike traditional digital assets, NFTs are unique and cannot be exchanged on a one-to-one basis, making them perfect for representing ownership or proof of authenticity.

Revolutionizing Healthcare Access and Privacy

With NFTs, the idea of securing and tracking the ownership of personal health records becomes a tangible reality. What I mean is that I could offer you a world where you have absolute control over your medical data.

CHAPTER 4.3

In this future, saying **Yes** to medical treatments, operations, or being part of scientific studies is as easy as clicking a button, getting rid of all the confusing paperwork.

Furthermore, the capacity for secure and anonymous data sharing through blockchain could revolutionize medical research, speeding up the creation of new treatments and therapies like never before.

Join me in this panoramic view, where the cosmos and technology meld, casting a vision where the flow of **secure data** lights the way to a future brimming with healing and discovery, all moving at the speed of thought across a **digital-organic-horizon**.

CHAPTER 4.4

Empowering Patients and Enhancing Engagement

Diving into how Non-Fungible Tokens (NFTs) can play a role in wellness programs has opened my eyes to an exciting trend: turning healthcare into a kind of game.

This adventure is about using the unique aspects of NFTs to create a healthcare journey that's not only engaging but also truly rewarding. Imagine earning NFTs by hitting health goals or joining in wellness challenges.

These challenges could be anything from completing fitness activities, sticking to your medication timetable, or engaging in practices to support your mental health.

The NFTs you earn are more than rewards; they're like digital medals of honor, celebrating your personal health achievements and encouraging you to take an active role in your wellness.

CHAPTER 4.4.1

Empowering Patients and Enhancing Engagement

But the perks of these NFTs go beyond just getting a pat on the back. Picture a world where collecting certain NFTs gives you keys to exclusive wellness workshops, personal health advice sessions, and even discounts on health products.

This setup doesn't just push you towards healthier habits; it customizes your health journey to align with your individual aims and likes, making the whole experience feel more tailored to you.

CHAPTER 4.5

Moreover, the community vibe that comes from these game-like elements is incredible. Sharing your wins and swapping or gifting NFTs creates a strong bond of support and encouragement.

Online platforms and social networks play a crucial role here, forming the foundation of a lively digital community where folks focused on health can thrive, share tips, and motivate each other.

Addressing Challenges and Ethical Considerations

As I navigate the vast possibilities of NFTs in enhancing patient engagement, I'm equally aware of the hurdles and ethical dilemmas that emerge.

Data privacy is a critical frontline issue. Employing blockchain to safeguard and manage health data and achievements demands strict compliance to data protection rules.

It's crucial to ensure that personal health information, even in its tokenized form, stays private and resistant to security breaches. My commitment to this isn't just about innovation; it's about upholding the highest standards of confidentiality and security for your health data.

CHAPTER 4.6

Towards a Future of Personalized Wellness

Delving into the transformative power of NFTs in healthcare, especially with the GAIA NFT Collection, I'm excited about a future where wellness becomes not just personalized but also securely managed.

This vision isn't just theoretical; it's becoming tangible, as demonstrated by projects like the **Medical Cannabis Holistic Center (MCHC)**, an innovative effort by the **Digital Quantum Association (DQA)**.

Harry | DQAvatar

CHAPTER 4.7

MCHC stands as a real-life example of what the GAIA NFTs Project envision: delivering customized healthcare services and wellness programs that incorporate the latest wellness insights, all securely backed by blockchain technology.

Yet, it's crucial to acknowledge that while MCHC is fully developed and poised to redefine our approach to healthcare, its worldwide introduction depends on obtaining the necessary funding.

Imagine a world where NFTs open doors to virtual wellness communities and provide personalized health advice through AI-driven platforms, or tokens that motivate us to keep up with our wellness routines, rewarding our commitment to health.

Through the **MultiversX** Blockchain's security and uniqueness, DQA is set to not only make healthcare more accessible but also to enable each of us to be an active participant in our wellness journey.

This pivotal moment for MCHC, a project under DQA, isn't just about unveiling a ready-to-deploy innovation; it's a call to action for all of us to support and realize this visionary healthcare model.

CHAPTER 4.8

To discover more about what MCHC could accomplish, check out www.mchc.io. There, the combination of blockchain, NFTs, and healthcare is not just a distant dream but a close reality, just waiting for that last bit of support to revolutionize wellness across the Planet.

Digital breakthroughs like blockchain and NFTs are ushering in a new healthcare era, moving us toward a future where wellness is tailored and empowering for all.

The shift from conventional healthcare to a digitized future opens doors to vast opportunities for improving health and happiness.

In conclusion

Wrapping up, we've journeyed through how digital tech, like blockchain and NFTs, is changing health and wellness. We're now at a big turning point in how we think about staying well.

This trip has shown us how technology can make healthcare more personal and better for everyone, pointing to a future where being healthy is an active, shared experience for all of us around the world.

CHAPTER 4.9

However, technology is just one piece of the wellness revolution puzzle. Another compelling narrative is unfolding across the European continent, one that promises to reshape our understanding
of natural therapies and their
place in modern healthcare systems.

This story is about our favorite plant that's been both celebrated and criticized, yet it has a long history in healing that dates back centuries.

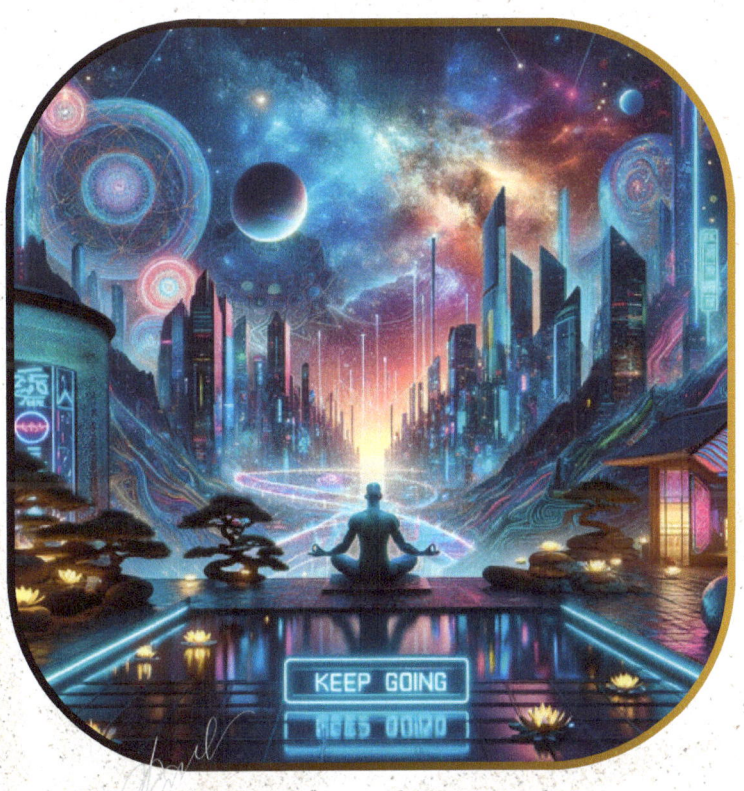

CHAPTER 5

Cannabis Expansion in Europe

A Green Revolution

As we transition from the digital world to the green landscapes of Europe, I'm thrilled to take you through the evolving saga of cannabis. Once relegated to the fringes of legality and social acceptance, it's now emerging into the limelight, showcasing not just its appeal for recreation but its profound potential for healing.

Europe is at the forefront of this green revolution, navigating a complex maze of regulations, shifting societal attitudes, and medical research. In this vibrant setting, enriched by centuries of history and cultural diversity, the narrative of cannabis is being rewritten.

In this chapter, we'll explore the dynamic journey of cannabis across European nations. We'll tackle the legal hurdles, ethical considerations, and the wider impact on society. The story of cannabis in Europe is as intricate and captivating as the continent itself.

CHAPTER 5.1

NFTVapeLab: A Glimpse into the Future

I will be introducing a unique venture, NFTVapeLab, birthed by Digital Quantum Association (DQA). This initiative is not just about advancing the commercial aspect of cannabis; it's about revolutionizing how we perceive and engage with this ancient herb through the lens of modern technology. Let's jump into it shall we...

The Regulatory Landscape - Europe's Mosaic of Policies

Shifting our gaze from the broad digital horizon to Europe's vibrant landscapes, I'm drawn into the complex world of cannabis regulation across the continent.

It's a mixture of different policies policies, where each country's stance on cannabis reflects its unique blend of culture, history, and societal values.

This diversity not only makes navigating the legal frameworks a challenge but also spotlights the evolving role of cannabis in our society.

CHAPTER 5.2

Take **The Netherlands, Germany,** and **Portugal,** for example. These countries are at the forefront, pioneering paths that integrate cannabis within their legal boundaries.

The Netherlands has long been a beacon of cannabis tolerance, offering a controlled, yet liberal, model through its famous Coffee Shops. This approach has not only stood the test of time but also offered valuable insights into regulated cannabis markets.

Then there's **Germany,** which recently made headlines by becoming the largest EU country to legalize cannabis for recreational use. This groundbreaking move allows for possession and cultivation under certain conditions, signaling a significant shift in drug policy and sparking a continent-wide conversation about public health, safety, and economic growth.

Portugal's model of decriminalization and harm reduction adds another layer to this narrative, showcasing the impact of treating drug use as a public health issue rather than a criminal one.

CHAPTER 5.3

My journey into the regulatory realms of Europe is enriched by our work with EU Partners and the insights from our Whitepaper.

These collaborations deepen our understanding of the regulatory landscape and its implications for healthcare, technology, and society.

Moreover, our involvement in the Europe Telemedicine Market points to a future where cannabis and healthcare innovation converge, promising more personalized and accessible care.

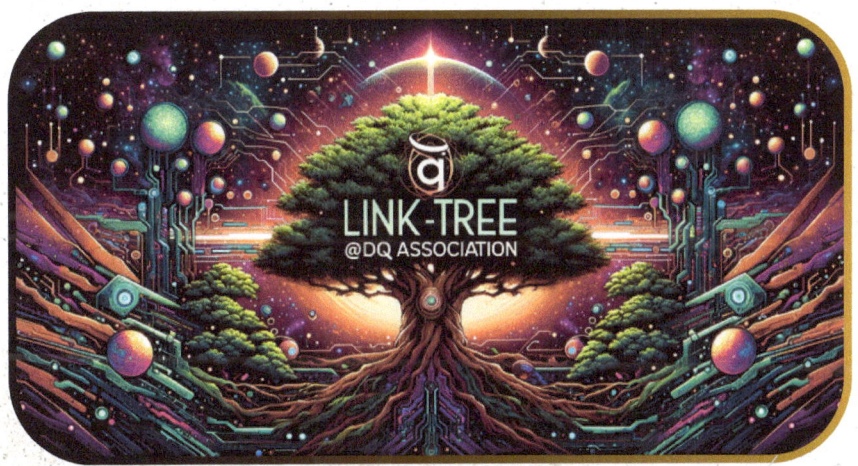

A Cosmic Cyberpunk tapestry where our 'Link-Tree @DQAssociation' shines brightly. This design marries the magic of nature with the allure of technology, creating a vivid and harmonious visual feast.

CHAPTER 5.4

With DQA's strategic development, we're setting our sights on significant expansion in Europe and beyond.

The telemedicine market in Europe is on the brink of explosive growth, projected to nearly double from USD 12.90 billion in 2020 to USD <u>24.84 billion</u> by 2028.

This growth represents a golden opportunity for us to integrate cannabis-based treatments into this burgeoning sector. Our revenue projections from 2024 to 2030 reflect this ambition, as we leverage partnerships across Europe for scalable expansion, aiming to establish a strong, enduring presence.

The recent shift in Germany underscores the changing tide of cannabis perception and regulation — a testament to the broader transformation underway across Europe. It highlights the need for ongoing dialogue and adaptability in integrating cannabis into our societies and economies.

CHAPTER 5.4.1

Navigating through Europe's complex regulatory landscape, it becomes evident that the continent's stance on cannabis is undergoing a transformation.

Observing the experiences of countries like the Netherlands, Germany, Portugal, and our joint initiatives, we glimpse a future where cannabis is not merely tolerated but integrated into the essence of wellness and healthcare.

Let me show you something...

CHAPTER 5.5

Cannabis Policy in Europe: An Overview
(Source: Forbes | Le Monde)

Countries with Legal Cannabis for Adult Use

- **Malta (2021):** The first EU country to legalize cannabis for adult use. Individuals are allowed to carry up to 7g and grow four plants at home. Cannabis purchases are facilitated through regulated, non-profit cooperatives.
- **Luxembourg (June 2023):** Legalized the personal possession and home cultivation of up to four cannabis plants per household for individuals 18 and older. Public possession, transportation, or purchasing of cannabis is still restricted.

Countries with Authorized Pilot Programmes

- **Switzerland:** Pioneered the pilot programme model for legal cannabis use, with several programs already operational or set to start in cities like Basel, Zürich, and Bern. These programmes aim to evaluate the impact of regulated cannabis sales on public health through studies conducted by partnering universities.

CHAPTER 5.6

- **The Netherlands:** Famous for its "Coffee Shops," the country initiated the "Wietexperiment" in December 2023. This allows in Dutch-Land a select number of licensed growers to supply cannabis to coffee shops in 10 cities, with the process subject to comprehensive monitoring and evaluation.

Proposed Legalization

- **Germany (Announced in 2022, Legalized April 1, 2024):** Initially announced its intention to legalize cannabis in 2022, culminating in becoming the largest EU country to legalize cannabis for recreational use by April 1, 2024. The German model includes provisions for personal use, home cultivation, and non-profit social clubs, with a commercial market introduction planned for future stages.

Czech Republic (Announced Last Year): Announced proposals for adult-use cannabis legalization, aiming for a comprehensive, regulated commercial market. Due to political opposition, current drafts focus on home cultivation and cannabis social clubs.

CHAPTER 5.7

Decriminalized Possession

- **Spain:** Decriminalized personal possession and cultivation, with the presence of over 1,000 cannabis social clubs, particularly in Barcelona.
- **Portugal (Since 2001):** Decriminalized possession of small quantities of all drugs. Specifically, up to 25g of cannabis herb or 5g of hashish is decriminalized.
- **Italy:** Decriminalized possession of small amounts for personal use and home cultivation, with continued penalties for sale.
- **Belgium (Since 2003):** Possession of up to 3g of cannabis or cultivation of one plant is considered a low priority for prosecution for individuals over 18.
- **Austria (Since 2016):** Decriminalized personal possession of cannabis, with an emphasis on individuals with no drug-related offenses within the last five years.

CHAPTER 5.7.1

Decriminalized Possession

- **Croatia:** Small amounts possession is a misdemeanor, subject to fines.
- **Estonia:** Up to 7.5g is deemed for personal use and punishable by a fine.
- **Slovenia:** Illegal, but possession of small amounts may be punished more leniently if individuals agree to enter a treatment or social welfare program.

CHAPTER 5.8

With a variety of models ranging from full legalization to pilot programmes and decriminalization, European countries are exploring different approaches to cannabis regulation, reflecting a continent-wide shift in drug policy.

Embrace the whispers of nature woven into the visage of the Earth; a richly detailed portrait blending a woman's face - GAIA's face, with rivers, trees and birds
the Avatar Tree

CHAPTER 5.9

Economic Ripple Effects of Cannabis Expansion

The legalization and decriminalization of Cannabis across various European countries are not just pivotal in terms of public health and social justice; they also unlock significant economic opportunities. The burgeoning cannabis market is set to catalyze growth and innovation across multiple sectors, from agriculture to technology and beyond.

Job Creation

The cannabis industry is a labor-intensive field at almost every stage of the supply chain — from cultivation and processing to distribution and retail.

As countries move towards a regulated cannabis market, there's a substantial increase in demand for a wide range of skills and occupations. These include agricultural roles, research and development, sales, marketing, and retail positions.

CHAPTER 5.9.1

Job Creation

Notably, the establishment of cannabis clubs and dispensaries necessitates a workforce for operations, creating numerous jobs and supporting local economies.

A futuristic cityscape at twilight, where the integration of cannabis clubs and dispensaries into the urban fabric symbolizes a new era of economic rejuvenation and social acceptance.

CHAPTER 5.1.0

Investment Opportunities

Legalization opens the door for both domestic and international investments. As cannabis markets mature and regulations become more defined, investors are increasingly drawn to the sector, attracted by the high growth potential. This influx of capital is crucial for innovation, expansion, and the overall scalability of cannabis businesses.

It also stimulates the broader economy, encouraging ancillary businesses such as security, legal services, and marketing firms to expand their services to cater to the cannabis industry.

Technological Advancement and NFTs

The intersection of cannabis and technology presents unique opportunities for innovation. Blockchain technology, in particular, has found a place in the cannabis industry through the use of non-fungible tokens (NFTs).

CHAPTER 5.1.1

NFTs can be utilized to verify the authenticity of cannabis products, trace product lifecycle from seed to sale, and even for marketing purposes.

For example, NFTs could represent ownership of a specific cannabis strain or limited-edition products, enhancing brand loyalty and customer engagement.

Additionally, technology plays a critical role in optimizing cultivation techniques, improving supply chain logistics, and ensuring compliance with regulations through track-and-trace systems.

CHAPTER 5.1.2

NFTVapeLab – Bridging Cannabis and Digital Innovation

Innovating Beyond Boundaries

NFTVapeLab.com stands at the confluence of cannabis culture and digital innovation. By leveraging NFTs to authenticate, celebrate, and distribute cannabis products, this project symbolizes a bold step forward.

NFTVapeLab **Drop-Shipping Platform**, in strategic integration with MCHC.io, our **Telemedicine Platform**, is set to revolutionize the CBD and Medical Cannabis market by introducing a pioneering business model that bridges the gap between health technology and Medical Cannabis wellness products.

Our mission is to deliver premium oils, vapes, and cosmetics, leveraging the efficiency of drop-shipping and the innovative potential of NFT technology.

CHAPTER 5.1.3

This unique ecosystem will provide a seamless experience from prescription to delivery, ensuring product efficacy and customer satisfaction.

With our GAIA NFT's you can unlock exclusive access to our platforms, raffles, giveaways, pre-sale pricing, and whitelist spots, along with premier telemedical and wellness tourism benefits.

GAIA NFT #65

CHAPTER 5.1.4

Once funded, our first commercial platform is all about our Drop-shipping business. Each NFT is a special pass, giving you access to lots of products and services.

Initial launch of our CBD & Medical Cannabis oil product line, capitalising on existing market demand & integration with the MCHC.io Telemedicine Platform within the first six months, enabling doctors to prescribe our products directly, thus significantly expanding our market reach. Introduction of CBD vapes and cosmetics over the following six months, aligning product launches with market readiness and legislative compliance.

Conclusion

The NFTVapeLab Drop-Shipping Platform, together with the MCHC.io Telemedicine Platform, represents a forward-thinking approach to wellness and healthcare.

By integrating high-quality CBD products with professional medical advice and innovative NFT technology, we are creating a new ecosystem that delivers personalized, efficient, and effective solutions to consumers worldwide.

CHAPTER 6

The Road Ahead

Envisioning a Future of Inclusion and Innovation

As we look to the future, the path of cannabis in Europe is one of potential and promise. The integration of digital solutions like NFTVapeLab signals a broader trend of acceptance and innovation.

Together, we stand on the brink of a new era where cannabis is not only accepted but embraced for its multiple benefits.

As we stand at the precipice of change, looking back on the journey we've embarked upon together, it's clear that the landscape of cannabis, technology, and healthcare is evolving more rapidly and inclusively than ever before.

This chapter isn't just a short conclusion but a gateway to the myriad possibilities that await us in a future rich with inclusion and innovation.

CHAPTER 6.1

I've deliberately kept our discussion centered on Europe, not touching on other areas. This decision reflects DQA's strategic priority on the European Union for 2024.

Other places matter, but they're not our focus right now. This shows where we're putting our energy and what we care about most.

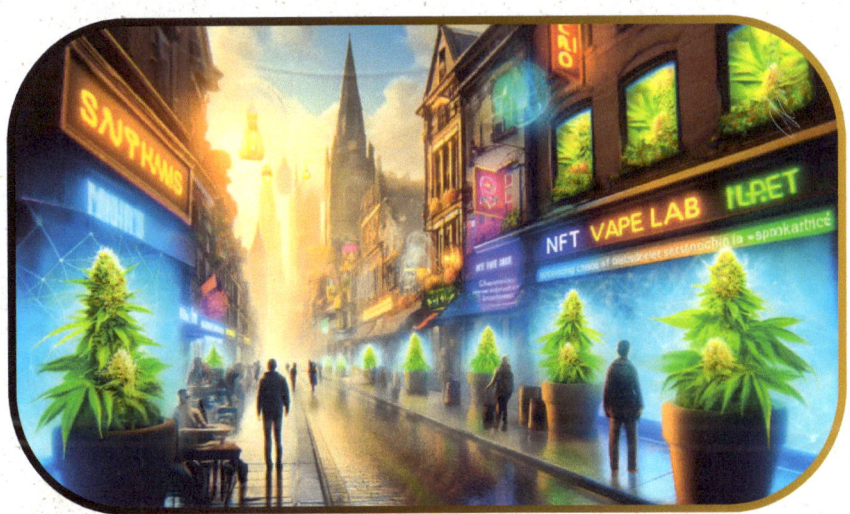

'Step' into a **Europe** where the essence of cannabis culture is interwind into the very fabric of society, enlightened by the digital glow of **NFTVapeLab**. This fusion of ancient wellness and futuristic innovation offers a glimpse into a world where harmony and health flourish under the banner
of progress and digital artistry.

CHAPTER 6.2

A New Dawn for Cannabis and Healthcare

We're at the start of something big with how cannabis is blending into Europe's health and wellness scene. This is just the opening act of a worldwide movement towards health practices that welcome everyone.

The push for legal cannabis, the growth of online health services, and breakthroughs like NFTs are coming together to forge a future where good health is a right for all, not a luxury.

Countries like the Netherlands, Germany, and Portugal are leading the way. They're showing us how to move into a future where we see cannabis and other natural treatments for what they truly offer, not through the lens of outdated judgments.

It's our boldness in questioning old ways, our willingness to explore the new, and our passion for making a difference that will keep us moving ahead.

CHAPTER 6.3

Innovation at the Intersection of Technology and Wellness

With the launch of projects like MCHC, NFTVapeLab and the growth of online health services, we're not just watching the cannabis scene change in healthcare; we're stepping into a brand-new era. This is where tech meets health in ways we never thought possible, and it's as big as we dare to dream.

Picture a world where your healthcare feels as tailored and easy to reach as your go-to online movie service. Imagine digital spaces not only offering health tips but also bringing people together, creating a place where everyone feels they belong.

In this world, NFTs aren't just for collecting or investing. They're keys to custom health experiences, connecting us with care providers over any distance, breaking down barriers.

CHAPTER 6.4

The Role of Community and Collective Action

As we look to the future, let's remember the crucial role of community and collective action. The discussions about cannabis, digital progress, and healthcare aren't just about individual decisions; they're about shaping our society as a whole.

Community power — whether online, on social media, or in local support circles — will be key in shaping the rules, tech, and habits that will define the next phase of wellness.

A Call to Action

Now, as we wrap up this chapter and turn our gaze to what lies ahead, I'm extending an invitation to you, our reader. Join me in this journey toward a future that's more inclusive and innovative. The path ahead might have obstacles, but it's also full of chances for us to grow, learn, and transform.

CONCLUSION

In "Wellness Reimagined: Cannabis, Digital Innovation, and the Future of Health," we've gone much further than just the usual health and technology talk.

I wrote every word wanting not just to tell you something, but to bring you into a new world of health that goes way past the old ways, into a future full of new ideas and personal change.

Looking back from the early days of cannabis to the latest in health-tech, I'm reminded of our first steps in "Navigating the Adult Industry, Cannabis, Crypto, and Beyond."

Our adventure wasn't just about seeing new things but really understanding how we and society can grow. It's been about seeing the strength we have to change what health and wellness mean, using both old wisdom and new possibilities.

CONCLUSION

Now, as we look forward, I ask you to think about the changes we've seen and been part of. Wellness isn't just about the past anymore; it's changing, influenced by what we've done, hoped for, and learned.

Our next step, "Navigating Personal Transformation: A Guide to Reinventing Your Life and Career," looks even more exciting. This new book is more than just a talk; it's a deeper dive into changing ourselves and our lives, in all ways.

et's take what we've learned, the insights we've gathered, and the connections we've made with us. We're at the start of a time when combining technology with traditional health practices will make wellness personal, easy to get to, and just right for everyone's own journey.

CONCLUSION

I'm not ending the conversation here but lighting a way to a future where health and happiness have no limits. As we move to the next part, I'm reaching out to you to come with me on this journey of change.

It's not just about facing the upcoming changes but about being the ones to shape a future where wellness and tech come together to open new doors.

Let's go into this next chapter with our hearts and minds open, ready for all the possibilities. The future of wellness isn't just a road we'll walk but a legacy we'll create, together.

I can't wait to keep going with you in "Navigating Personal Transformation: A Guide to Reinventing Your Life and Career."

Together, let's redefine the future.

REVOLUTION ROAD #5
Q2 2024

RCS

BEYOND BOUNDARIES

www.ingramcontent.com/pod-product-compliance
Lightning Source LLC
Chambersburg PA
CBHW040233220526
45473CB00001B/222